God Truly Exists

Here's The Proof

JAMES A. SURRELL, M.D.

GOD TRULY EXISTS
Here's The Proof

James A. Surrell, M.D.

Published by
BEAN BOOKS, LLC, Newberry, Michigan
sosdietdoc@gmail.com

Designed by Stacey Willey of
Globe Printing, Ispeming, Michigan
www.globeprinting.net

Cover Art by Sandi Mager

ISBN # 978-0-9825601-1-2

DEDICATION
This book is dedicated all my very special family and friends, and to all of the wonderful people of the Upper Peninsula of Michigan.

TABLE OF CONTENTS

DEFINITIONS

INCORRUPT - Incorruptibility is a divine intervention that allows some human bodies to completely or partially avoid the normal process of body decomposition after death as a sign of their holiness.

STIGMATA - Bodily wounds that appear in the same locations as the crucifixion wounds of Jesus Christ that were on His hands, chest wall and feet.

INTRODUCTION

Perhaps one of the most important questions ever asked is the following. "Does God really exist... and if so, what is the proof?" In my judgment, this represents the most significant question we could ever ask ourselves or ask others. Clearly, this is a profound question that certainly deserves an enlightened answer. Yes, there is an overwhelming amount of proof that God does indeed exist. So, let's take a look at just some of this proof that we can really focus on, easily understand, and share with others.

Let us now reflect on this great question about the existence of God and review just some of the monumental proof that allows us to prepare an appropriate answer. What if we could truly look at a number of readily available items that, in my humble judgment, offer absolutely unmistakable, completely undeniable, and easily understood proof of the existence of God? Well, my friends, many such items are awaiting our personal review. Let's take a look at just a few items that have withstood the test of time over many centuries that clearly do offer such undeniable proof of the existence of God and his beloved Son, Jesus Christ.

Before we begin, please understand that to become a doubly board-certified surgeon, I had to first become a medical doctor and learn to become true scientist. In this regard, a physician is thoroughly trained to maintain a healthy skepticism and to always carefully assess any information we receive to be certain it is based on truth that can be verified, and not merely based on someone's opinion. This is how we will approach the following evidence that proves, beyond any doubt, of the existence of our God.

CHAPTER 1
Incorrupt Bodies of Saints

I remain totally in awe over the concept of incorrupt bodies of about 200 Catholic Saints. As a medical scientist, I know that this just cannot happen. There is absolutely no way that human body tissue will not decay over a number of years, let alone over a number of centuries! That is, of course, unless a true miracle from God has occurred. Many of the incorrupt (not decayed) bodies of Saints may be viewed in various locations in France, Italy, the Vatican, and at other locations as well. Below is a 1999 photograph taken of the incorrupt body of Saint Bernadette Soubirous. Her incorrupt body may be viewed in the Chapel of St. Bernadette in Nevers, France. Saint Bernadette died in 1879 and her body remains completely intact (incorrupt) after more than 100 years.

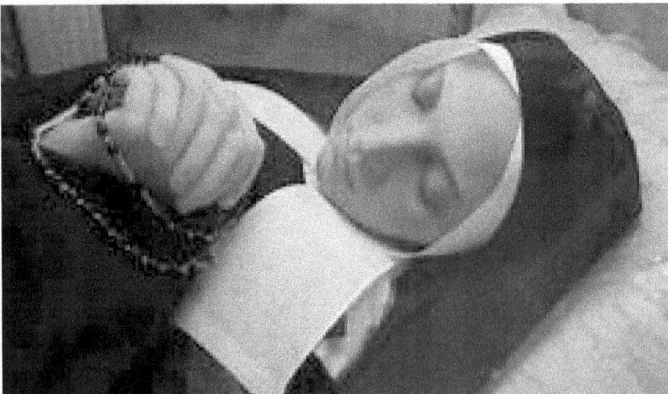

SAINT BERNADETTE SOUBIROUS,
INCORRUPT BODY (BODY NEVER DECAYED)

CHAPTER 2
The Parting of the Red Sea

We are told in The Book of Exodus 14 from the Old Testament of the Bible that Moses and the Israelites were fleeing the Egyptians who were pursuing them to kill them. To escape, Moses was able to part the waters of the Red Sea, and safely reach the other side of the Red Sea before they could be attacked and slaughtered. Then, when the Egyptian Army followed them into the parted waters of the Red Sea, the water closed down upon the Egyptians riding their chariots, and they were all killed. Is this just some fable that has been repeated through the years, or is there conclusive evidence to confirm the historical accuracy of this Biblical teaching? There is photographic evidence of both human and horse bones and chariot wheels in the Red Sea. I find the following photo of a chariot wheel on the bottom of the Red Sea to be rather compelling evidence of proof that the Egyptians were indeed trapped and drowned as the waters of the Red Sea closed down upon them.

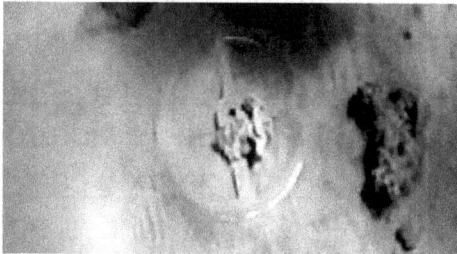

Chariot Wheel on the Bottom of the Red Sea

CHAPTER 3
Prophecy Fulfillment

Generally, a Biblical prophecy is defined as a prediction of an event that will happen perhaps many hundreds of years later. When a significant event happens that was precisely predicted many centuries earlier, this must be also viewed as yet another proof of the existence of God. Many scholars have evaluated the statistical odds of a significant historical event happening exactly as predicted centuries earlier. The conclusion always comes down to the fact that this could not happen by chance, and that it truly represents a God-inspired prophecy.

For example, the Bible tells us that Jesus spoke these words from the Cross during his Crucifixion. "My God, My God, why hast thou forsaken me?" What is not generally appreciated is that these are the first words of Psalm 22, which he was speaking out loud. Further, it is important to note that Psalm 22:16 and Psalm 22:18 contain very specific prophecies telling what would happen to the Messiah on the day of His Crucifixion. Psalm 22:16 – For dogs have surrounded me; a band of evildoers has encompassed me; they have pierced my hands and my feet. Psalm 22:18 – They divide my garments among them; for my clothing they cast lots. Please take note that Psalm 22 was written approximately 1000 years before the Crucifixion and it contains these very specific prophecies that His hands and feet would be pierced and that those soldiers doing the crucifixion would cast lots to see who would get His clothes. All of these events surrounding the coming of the true Messiah were predicted and documented in the 22nd Psalm a thousand years before they actually took place. Clearly, the writing of this Psalm 1000 years earlier containing these prophecies could only have been written through divine inspiration from God.

CHAPTER 4
The Stigmata (Wounds of Christ) on Padre Pio

Padre Pio was born on May 25, 1887, in Pietrelcina, Italy, a small country town in Southern Italy. He passed away on September 23, 1968. He was named a Saint by Pope John Paul II on June 2, 2002. On September 20, 1918, while praying in the choir loft of his church, Padre Pio received his visible Stigmata (the five wounds of Christ), which would stay with him for the remaining 50 years of his devoted religious life. The wounds of Christ on his hands could be seen when he said Mass and by early 1919, word of his Stigmata spread to the outside world.

Over the years countless people, including physicians, examined Padre Pio's wounds. Padre Pio was really not interested in the physicians' attempts to explain his Stigmata. He accepted it as a gift from God, though he would have preferred to suffer the pains of Christ's Passion without the world knowing.

Saint Padre Pio is perhaps best known today as the first priest to demonstrate the Crucifixion wounds of Christ on his hands, feet and right side of his chest when he said Mass. This has been thoroughly documented by numerous photographs and thorough medical evaluations and of course, can only be explained as a gift of the Stigmata given to the very devout Padre Pio. Clearly, the stigmata of

Padre Pio clearly represents even more thoroughly documented proof of the existence of God. He passed away in 1968, more than 50 years ago, and his body has not decayed at all and is also considered to be incorrupt.

STIGMATA ON PADRE PIO
(THE FIVE WOUNDS OF CHRIST)

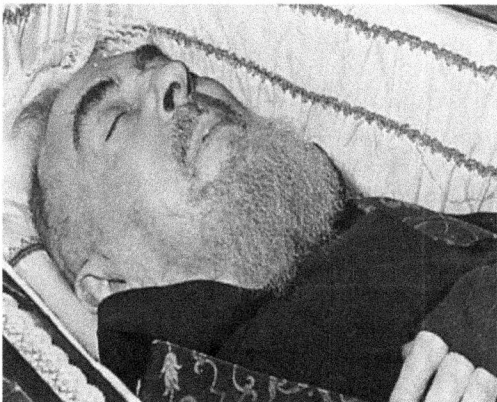

INCORRUPT BODY OF SAINT PADRE PIO
(BODY NEVER DECAYED)

CHAPTER 5
The Cloak of Saint Juan Diego

The cloak (also called a tilma) of Saint Juan Diego is made of cactus cloth fiber. It would be expected that this ancient fabric might last up to twenty years before it starts to disintegrate and fall apart. This is the cloak that Juan Diego was wearing when our Blessed Virgin Mary appeared to him in the year 1531 and told him to go speak to the Bishop of Mexico and tell him to build a church on this remote site. He then dutifully went to see the Bishop, and was able to get an audience with the Bishop. The bishop did not believe for a moment that this poor Aztec Indian Juan Diego had just had a visitation from the Blessed Virgin Mary. He then dismissed him with the charge to come back with some proof that he had been visited by our Blessed Mother. Our Blessed Mother again appeared to Juan Diego and imposed the image of herself on his cloak as proof for the Bishop. When Juan Diego went back to the Bishop and he saw this image, it was then very clear that the Bishop was to build a new Catholic church on this site. After this event, it is estimated that 9 million natives were converted to Christianity over the next twenty years.

The tilma, or cloak, of Juan Diego remains intact to this day and is on display at the Basilica of Guadalupe in Mexico City. This Basilica is visited by up to 20 million people every year, making it one of the most visited Christian sites in the world. Unbeliev-ably, this cactus cloth tilma remains completely intact after nearly 500 years. Of course, the cloak of Juan Diego should have completely deteriorated into dust more than 450 years ago. It remains on display in Mexico City today. This too is a miracle and can only be explained by miraculous intervention, offering even more proof of the existence of God.

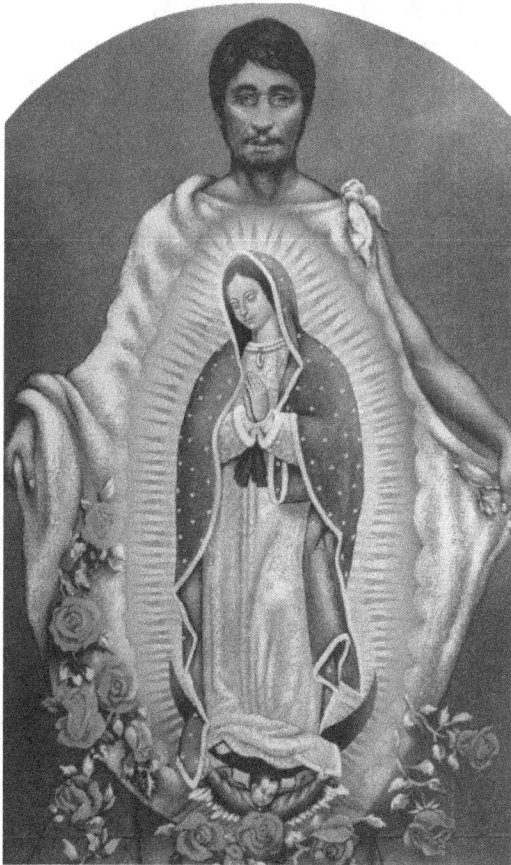

Image of Blessed Mother on Juan Diego Tilma
(See color image of this on the back cover.)

CHAPTER 6
Miraculous Sparing of the
Statue of Blessed Mary in Spain

On July 30, 2015, a statue of the Blessed Virgin Mary survived a major fire at a military base in Spain. During a very severe heat wave in Spain, this fire broke out at the El Goloso military base, near Madrid. Of course, the fire destroyed all in its path. Eventually, the fire fighting personnel got this fire under control and when they were able to get to the center of it, they were shocked and absolutely amazed. There they found a completely spared and undamaged statue of Our Lady of Lourdes, along with the surrounding beautiful undamaged flowers.

Blessed Mary Statue Completely
Unharmed by the Fire

CHAPTER 7
Miraculous Survival of the
Hiroshima Atomic Bomb Blast

On August 6, 1945, nearly 80 years ago, eight Jesuit Priests were living in a home in Hiroshima, Japan. They lived less than one mile away from ground zero, which is the point of impact where the atomic bomb landed in Hiroshima. Miraculously, all eight Priests survived the atomic blast. Everyone else who was anywhere near the ground zero point of impact of this atomic bomb was reported to have died instantly. Many more people, who were not instantly killed from the bomb blast died from nuclear radiation within just a few days.

These eight surviving Priests were examined over 200 times by physicians and multiple medical scientists. Not one of them experienced any physical or radiation injury. These Priests were questioned many times in attempts to explain their completely miraculous survival. Every time the Priests were questioned, they repeated the same explanation for their survival, "We believe that we survived because we were living the Divine Message of Fatima. We lived and prayed the Rosary daily in our home."

CHAPTER 8
The Shroud of Turin

The Shroud is a linen cloth woven in a 3-over-1 herringbone pattern, and measures 14' 3" x 3' 7". These dimensions are completely consistent with loom technology of the period. The finer weave of 3-over-1 herringbone is consistent with the New Testament statement that the shroud was purchased by Joseph of Arimathea, who was a wealthy man.

THE FACE OF JESUS THAT REMAINS ON THE SHROUD OF TURIN

Italian scientists conducted Shroud experiments between 2005 and 2010, applying ultraviolet radiation to strips of linen to see if they could match the coloration on the fibers of the Shroud of Turin. They found that these doses of radiation left a thin coating on linen fibers that resemble the colored fibers on the image of the Shroud of Turin. These findings support the idea that the image on the Shroud was made by a sudden flash of high-energy radiation.

The bloodstains on the Shroud are from clotted wounds transferred to the cloth by contact with a wounded human body. The blood on the Shroud is type AB human male blood. This blood type is rare (about 3% of the world population). Dr. Alan Adler and Dr. John Heller of the New England Institute of Medicine found a high concentration of the pigment bilirubin, consistent with someone dying under great stress or trauma. Doctors from the University of Texas Health Science Center found X & Y chromosomes representing male blood and "degraded DNA" consistent with this being ancient blood.

The image on the Shroud is of a man 5 feet 10 1/2 inches tall, about 175 pounds, covered with scourge wounds and blood stains. Numerous highly respected world-wide surgeons and pathologists have studied the match between the weapons used by the Roman soldiers, and the wounds described in the Bible. These noted scientists all agree that the words of the New Testament clearly match the wounds depicted on the Shroud, consistent with the weapons used by ancient Roman soldiers in Crucifixion.

Further, the scourge marks on the shoulders, back, and legs of the Man of the Shroud clearly match the expected injuries from a Roman whip which has three leather thongs, each having two lead or bone pellets on the end. The lance wound in the right side matches the Roman 4 cm. x 1 cm. spear wound. The wrist wounds are from the 7 inch Iron nails used by the Romans for Crucifixion. These documented injuries, combined with the capping of thorns offer even more compelling proof of this Shroud being the true burial cloth of the crucified body of Jesus of Nazareth.

SUMMARY

Each and every one of the eight items briefly reviewed in this book offers overwhelming and totally undeniable evidence for the existence of God. When looked at from a critical and impartial standpoint, it should be exceedingly clear that not one of these eight events could ever have occurred without divine guidance and intervention. When reviewed individually, any one of these eight items offers a monumental and compelling amount of evidence that clearly proves the existence of God.

Following is a very brief overview of these eight items that offer very compelling evidence and absolute proof of the existence of our God.

1. **Incorrupt Bodies of Saints** – There is absolutely no way to scientifically explain how the remains of a deceased human will not decay over time. This can only take place as a miracle from God.

2. **The Parting of the Red Sea** – Multiple sources have confirmed the presence of ancient chariot wheels and human and horse bones on the bottom of the Red Sea. This confirms this Biblical truth.

3. **Prophecy Fulfillment** – A very significant historical event that happens precisely as it was predicted to happen 1000 years earlier cannot happen by chance. These prophecies are divinely inspired by God.

4. **The Stigmata on Padre Pio** – The exact replication of the Crucifixion wounds of Christ could only have been placed on Padre Pio by divine intervention. There is no other scientific medical explanation.

5. **The Tilma of Juan Diego** – This cactus fiber tilma (cloak) of Juan Diego with the image of Blessed Mary has not deteriorated over nearly 500 years. This clearly represents a miraculous preservation.

6. **Miraculous sparing of Blessed Mary Statue** – The only possible explanation of the sparing of this statue of Our Lady of Lourdes in the middle of this significant fire is from Divine Intervention from God.

7. **Miraculous Survival of Eight Priests at the Hiroshima Atomic Bomb Blast** – The survival of these eight Priests near ground zero of the Hiroshima atomic bomb blast can only be explained as a result of miraculous intervention from God. Their survival truly was a miracle from God.

8. **The Shroud of Turin** – All the scientifically documented injuries noted on the Shroud offer very compelling proof of this Shroud being the true burial cloth of the crucified body of Jesus of Nazareth.

APPENDIX A – LETTERS IN WORDS_
Suggested possible meanings
for the letters in various words (acronyms).
(In Alphabetical Order)

ANGELS
= Always Near, Guarding Every Living Soul

ASAP = Always Say A Prayer

ASK = Ask, Seek, Knock (In the Bible twice at
Matthew 7:7 and Luke11:9)

BIBLE = Basic Instruction Before Leaving Earth

CHRIST
= Christians Have Rewards In Spiritual Treasures

FAITH = Faith Always Is The Hope

FAMILY = Father And Mother, I Love You

FEAR = False Evidence Appearing Real

FOCUS = Focus On Christ, our Ultimate Savior

GIFT = God's Instructions For Thanksgiving

GROWTH = God Reveals Our Way To Heaven

GUARDIANS = Guarding Us All, Ready to Deliver In All New Situations

HOPE = Help Other People Everywhere

JESUS = Jesus, our Eternal Savior for Ultimate Salvation

LIFE = Love Is For Everybody

LOVE = Love Others, Value Everybody

NOW = No Other Way

OTHERS = Offer To Help Everybody, Respectfully and Sincerely

PUSH = Pray Until Something Happens

WORDS = Welcome Others with Respect, Dignity, and Sincerity

APPENDIX B – PRAYERS ARE ANSWERED
(Just as He Promised)

P.U.S.H. → Pray Until Something Happens

"Lord, teach us to pray." – Luke 11:1

"This, then, is how you should pray: Our Father in heaven, hallowed be your name." – Matthew 6:9

"And all things you ask in prayer, believing, you will receive." – Matthew 21:22

"I will do whatever you ask in my name, so that the Father may be glorified in the Son. If in my name you ask me for anything, I will do it." – John 14:13-14

"If you remain in me and my words remain in you, ask whatever you wish, and it will be given you." – John 15:7

"Therefore I tell you, whatever you ask for in prayer, believe that you have received it, and it will be yours." – Mark 11:24

The wisdom from the following same two teachings from Jesus about prayer appear in both Matthew and Luke.

"Ask and it will be given to you; seek and you shall find; knock and the door will be opened to you. For everyone who asks receives; he who seeks finds; and to him who knocks, the door will be opened." – Matthew 7:7-8

"So I say to you, ask, and it will be given to you; seek, and you will find; knock, and it will be opened to you. For everyone who asks receives, and he who seeks finds, and to him who knocks, it will be opened." – Luke 11:9-10

It is amazing that these promises from Jesus about prayer make up the very word: "**ASK**".

A - **A**sk, and it will be given to you...
S - **S**eek, and you will find...
K - **K**nock, and the door will be opened to you...

"But when you pray, go into your room, close the door and pray to your Father, who is unseen. Then your Father, who sees what is done in secret, will reward you." – Matthew 6:6

"The prayer of a righteous man is powerful and effective." – James 5:16

"Do not be anxious about anything, but in everything, by prayer and petition, with thanksgiving, present your requests to God. And the peace of God, which transcends all understanding, will guard your hearts and your minds in Christ Jesus."
– Philippians 4:6-7

"I can do all things through Christ who gives me strength." – Philippians 4:13

"For I know the plans I have for you, declares the LORD, plans to prosper you and not to harm you, plans to give you hope and a future." – Jeremiah 29:11

About Your Author
JAMES A. SURRELL, M.D.

Fellow, American College of Surgeons
Fellow, American Society of
Colon and Rectal Surgeons

Dr. Surrell is a board certified colorectal surgeon and holds fellowship status in both the American Society of Colon and Rectal Surgeons and the American College of Surgeons. In addition to his best selling "SOS (Stop Only Sugar) Diet" book, Dr. Surrell has published numerous additional books, including: "The ABC's For Success In All We Do", "The Human Digestive System Owner's Manual", "Laughter Is Good Medicine", "Talk With The Doc", "Your ABC's For Patriotism, and "Handbook for Easy Weight Loss & Nutritional Health". He has also authored many articles in various medical journals.

With regard to his assessment and conclusions noted in this book, Dr. Surrell has a very extensive history of critically and scientifically looking at multiple sources of information for his many books. Be assured that he also looked very carefully at each of the eight issues documented in this book offering undeniable proof of the existence of our God.

www.ingramcontent.com/pod-product-compliance
Lightning Source LLC
Chambersburg PA
CBHW061654050426
42443CB00027B/3299